The Crusades Explained

The English Reading

Keith Goodman

Published by G-L-R (Great Little Read)

Copyright: The English Reading Tree/GLR

This book is sold subject to the condition that it shall not by way of trade or otherwise be resold or hired out or otherwise circulated without the written or verbal consent of the author.

Written by Keith Goodman

Reading Age for this book: 9+

The reading age for the series will vary but starts at seven

The English Reading Tree Series has been written for children aged seven and over. It is the perfect tool for parents to get their children into the habit of reading.

This book has been created to entertain and educate young minds and is packed with information and trivia and lots of authentic images that bring the topic alive.

There is a quiz at the end to test how much has been learned

TABLE OF CONTENTS

What Were the Crusades?..6

The First Crusade..8

The Second Crusade 11

The Third Crusade 14

The Fourth Crusade 17

The Children's Crusade 19

The Fifth Crusade 22

The Sixth Crusade 24

The Seventh Crusade 26

The Eighth Crusade 29

The Ninth Crusade 31

Crusades Trivia...34

Crusades Quiz...37

Thank you for Reading this Book...38

Crusades Quiz Answers..42

Attributions 43

What Were the Crusades?

Jerusalem

The Crusades took place over a two-hundred-year period during the Middle Ages. They were a series of campaigns between Christians from Europe and Muslims in the Middle East. The fighting was for control of Jerusalem, a city in the Holy Land special to both religions.

The city of Jerusalem, located in the Middle East, was important to several religions for different reasons.

For the Jewish religion, it was where King Solomon built a temple to God.

For Muslims, Jerusalem is where the Prophet Muhammad ascended to Heaven.

For Christians, it is where Jesus was crucified and rose from the dead.

Starting in 1095, the Crusades took place over the next two hundred years, with European Christian Armies invading the Middle East (Holy Land) to capture the city of Jerusalem.

This is the story of the Crusades and the people who fought in them

The First Crusade

During Medieval times (Middle Ages), the Muslim Empire stretched from India to Spain and included Jerusalem and the Holy Land.

Even though Jerusalem was under Islamic control, Christian pilgrims were not harmed when they visited the city. In 1077, all of this changed as Seljuk Turks gained control of the Holy Land.

From 1077, it became harder for Christian pilgrims to travel around the Holy Land.

There was fear that the Turks would attack the Christian city of Constantinople, and the Pope promised Christian knights in Europe forgiveness for their sins if they went on a Crusade to win Jerusalem back.

The response was incredible, and many people, both rich and poor, sewed red crosses onto their clothes and set off to the Holy Land to do 'God's work.'

The First Crusade started in 1096, and people from Italy, France, and Germany set off on the long journey to Jerusalem, led by nobles and knights.

After surrounding the city of Jerusalem, the army from Europe captured it in 1099.

Losing the holy city of Jerusalem was a terrible blow to Muslims, but for the Christians back in Europe, it was hailed as a fantastic success.

Holding on to Jerusalem was difficult even though a Christian kingdom had been established around the city.

The Second Crusade

After the achievement of the First Crusade, Christian states were established in the Middle East. These were:

- The Kingdom of Jerusalem
- The Principality of Antioch
- The County of Edessa
- The County of Tripoli

The weakest and most northerly of these states was the County of Edessa. This had the smallest population and was constantly being attacked by Muslim troops.

The Second Crusade was started in 1147. It was a military response to the overthrow of the County of Edessa in 1144. Edessa was established during the First Crusade by King Baldwin of Jerusalem in 1098.

It was the first Middle Eastern Christian State to be founded but the first to be overthrown.

The Second Crusade came after a call to arms by Pope Eugene III and was led by King Conrad III of Germany and King Louis VII of France.

The two armies marched separately to the Holy Land, and each was defeated by the Seljuk Turks.

The Second Battle of Dorylaeum took place during the Second Crusade in October 1147. It was not one battle but a series of skirmishes between Turkish and German troops over several days.

The German Army under Conrad III was, eventually, heavily defeated by the Seljuk Turks under Sultan Mesud I

The French Army, with some survivors from the defeated German Army, had some minor victories against Muslim forces but was heavily defeated as it approached the city of Antioch.

After a disastrous attempt at taking the city of Damascus, the remaining Crusaders headed for home, though many never made. They were either killed by Muslim soldiers or by disease.

The Second Crusade was a huge Islamic victory and would have a big influence on the recapture of Jerusalem by Islamic Armies, and the Third Crusade

The Third Crusade

There was yet another call to arms in 1189 after a Muslim Army under Sultan Saladin defeated Christian knights at the Battle of Hattin and captured Jerusalem.

The Third Crusade started in 1189 and was led by three European monarchs. These were:

- Philip II of France
- Richard (the Lionheart) I of England

- Frederick (Barbarossa) I, the Holy Roman Emperor.

The third Crusade is also called the Kings' Crusade.

This Crusade was slightly more successful than the Second Crusade, as the Christian Army did recapture the cities of Jaffa and Acre, but the ultimate goal of Jerusalem was never a real possibility.

The aging, German, Frederick Barbarossa, led a huge German Army through Eastern Europe and did win some minor battles against the Turks. However, on June 10, 1190, the weight of his armor caused him to drown while crossing a river. He never got to the Holy Land, and neither did most of his soldiers. In despair at the death of their leader, lots of them went home.

Leopold of Austria replaced Frederick Barbarossa at the head of the German troops, and with the help of Philip of France and Richard the Lionheart, they attacked the city of Acre in June 1191. The city was taken on June 11, but the army leaders quarreled, and Philip and Leopold took their armies home. This left Richard the Lionheart on his own to fight Saladin.

In December 1191, only twelve miles from Jerusalem, Richard, and his Army were forced to retreat due to appalling weather conditions.

It became clear that Richard I would have difficulty taking and holding onto Jerusalem, but it was also clear that Saladin was not sure that he could defeat the Crusaders.

A peace was agreed. Saladin would keep Jerusalem, but unarmed Christian pilgrims could visit the city in safety.

Neither the Muslims nor the Christians were satisfied with the conclusion of the Third Crusade.

Richard had succeeded in keeping hold of the coastal areas but was criticized in Europe for failing to take Jerusalem.

The Islamic world was unhappy because Saladin had failed to drive the Crusaders out of the Holy Land.

The Fourth Crusade

The conquest of Constantinople

In 1202, Pope Innocent III came up with the idea to attack the Holy Land by going through Egypt and then capturing Jerusalem.

There was still outrage in Europe that Jerusalem had not been taken.

Unfortunately, the city of Venice was commissioned to provide the ships to transport the army to the Middle East. This proved to be a problem that led to the plan's failure.

The plan seemed simple enough, but it had to be changed drastically by involving the Venetians. The Crusaders could not pay the Venetians for transport by sea, as they didn't have enough money. The Venetians asked them to help attack a couple of cities as payment. One of them was the beautiful Christian city of Constantinople, and the other was the city of Zara (called Zadar in modern-day Croatia).

After the successful attack against Zara in November 1202, the city of Constantinople was attacked and looted by Crusaders in 1204

It looked like the idea of the Crusades had changed drastically since the First Crusade in 1096, as both Constantinople and Sara were Christian cities.

The Children's Crusade

There was still a lot of enthusiasm in Europe to take Jerusalem back from the control of the Muslims. By 1212, this religious enthusiasm was so strong that it inspired what is now known as the Children's Crusade.

The Children's Crusade was not only children but was made up of impoverished people, the old, the sick, and many young people. This was a crusade of ordinary people from Germany and France, and it never had official approval from the nobles or the Catholic Church.

A young shepherd boy from Cloyes in France called Stephen claimed that Jesus had come to him in a vision. News of the boy and his vision spread to Germany, and it was here that Nicholas of Cologne banded together children to join with Stephen and head for the Holy Land.

It was believed that God would part the Mediterranean Sea and allow the children's army to walk to the Holy Land.

Many made it to Genoa in Italy, and from here, little is known about what happened. Very few made it home, and it was claimed that corrupt merchants sold many into slavery. It is also very probable that some found work and stayed in Italy.

Figures are vague about how many people took part in the Children's Crusade, but it was probably between fifteen and thirty thousand.

The Fifth Crusade

The crusaders used machines to hurl rocks at the walls of besieged cities

Pope Innocent III called for another Crusade to capture Jerusalem in 1217. Having seen how most of the other crusades had failed, this

Crusade aimed to attack Muslim cities in Egypt. The plan was to march on Jerusalem as soon as they had conquered Egypt.

The Crusaders succeeded in taking the important Muslim city of Damietta, but defeat at the hands of a Muslim Army, disease, and leadership squabbles meant that Damietta could not be held.

Like every other Crusade since the first, the Christian Army left for home, having achieved very little.

The Sixth Crusade

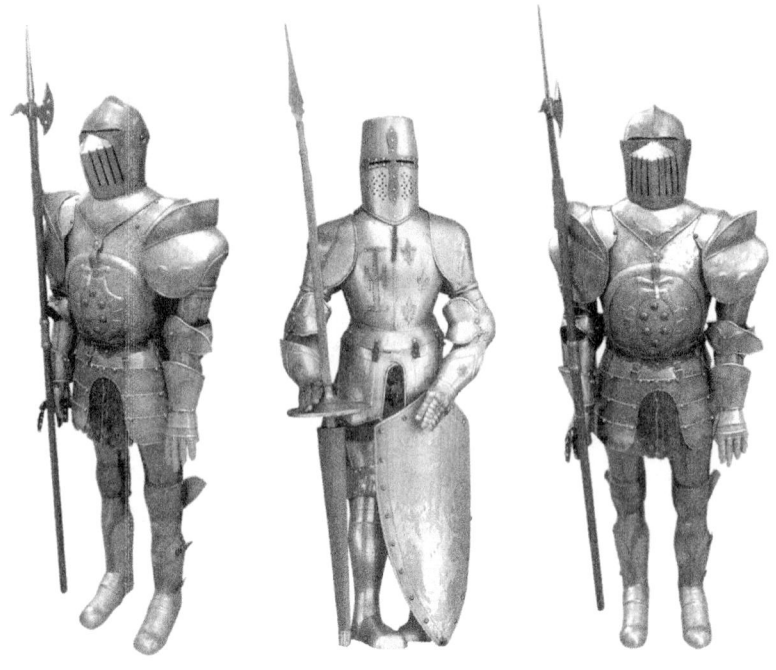

Imagine how hot armor would have been to wear in battle

The Sixth Crusade is also called the Crusade of Frederick II. It took place in 1228, just seven years after the disastrous fifth crusade. Like all other crusades, the main aim was to recapture the Holy Land and Jerusalem.

Frederick was the Holy Roman Emperor and had taken a vow during his coronation to take back Jerusalem

The Crusader Army went by sea to the Christian-held city of Acre and planned to advance and take control of the city of Jerusalem.

The reality of the situation was that the Christian Army was neither big enough nor strong enough to complete the task of capturing the holy city. Frederick II was well aware of this and hoped for some kind of negotiated access.

The Egyptian Sultan, Al-Kamil, agreed to surrender Jerusalem after some complicated talks with the Christian leader.

Frederick marched with his army into Jerusalem on March 17, 1229. The Sixth Crusade though successful, was still not as successful as the First Crusade, and the negotiations only guaranteed the Christian control of the city for ten years. This would eventually see the situation reverting to Muslim rule and more Crusades.

The Seventh Crusade

King Louis IX of France

Jerusalem came back under Muslim control in 1244. The situation in Europe was not good for the start of a new and costly campaign to the Holy Land.

By 1244, the people of Europe had grown tired of the Crusades, and the constant fighting between the great European powers meant that the kings were more interested in taking land off each other than retaking Jerusalem.

While the idea of taking an army to the Holy Land was not met with enthusiasm, there were still people who were outraged enough to start pushing for the Seventh Crusade.

It was Louis IX of France that answered the call.

In 1244, France was one of the strongest nations in Europe, and Louis didn't have a problem finding the money to pay for the Crusade.

As well as the king, there were a lot of French nobles that wanted to reclaim Jerusalem.

The French King left for the Holy Land with 3,000 knights in a force of 15,000 well-armed Crusaders.

They left the South of France in 36 transport ships and arrived in Egypt in 1249. The king and his large army were in high spirits and were confident that they could capture Jerusalem.

The Crusaders captured the Egyptian city of Damietta, with the Muslim forces fleeing before them. However, the River Nile flooded its banks and left the king and his men stranded in the city for the next six months.

When he was eventually able to leave, Louis marched on the city of Cairo. Here, he suffered a heavy defeat and was forced to retreat to Damietta in 1250.

Louis was eventually taken prisoner, and his army destroyed.

The Seventh Crusade ended with the king being ransomed and being allowed to return to France in 1254.

The Seventh Crusade had promised a lot, but it had achieved nothing.

The Eighth Crusade

The Seventh Crusade didn't capture the holy city and failed to hold on to any meaningful territory in the Holy Land. This included the Egyptian city of Damietta.

In 1270, The French King Louis IX led the Eighth Crusade to recapture Jerusalem.

Louis IX had never stopped believing that it was his destiny to enter Jerusalem at the head of his army and open it up again for Christian pilgrims to travel safely.

On March 24th, 1267, King Louis announced that it was his intention once again to 'take the cross.'

The plan for the Eighth Crusade was to capture the city of Tunis in North Africa and use it as a port to attack Egypt.

The king and his army set up camp by the walls of the city of Tunis and waited for more soldiers to arrive.

Many of the Crusaders became ill with dysentery, and many died. Unfortunately, for the Crusade, this included King Louis IX. He died in August 1270.

This ended the Eighth Crusade as the survivors returned home.

The Ninth Crusade

The Ninth Crusade followed the Eighth Crusade almost immediately.

The leader of this Crusade was Lord Edward of England, who was to become King Edward I. Edward 'took the cross' in June 1268 and left to meet with Louis IX at the siege of Tunis.

When Edward got to Tunis and realized that the King of France was dead, he continued to the Holy Land with his small army.

This was the Ninth Crusade.

Lord Edward arrived at Acre in August 1271. This city had been a Christian stronghold for over two hundred years but had been threatened by Muslim forces.

Edward wanted to help the city of Acre, even though he only had around three hundred knights and about seven hundred soldiers.

The arrival of Edward saw the Muslim forces retreat, and in the months that followed, Edward and his men won several small battles against the Muslims.

One of Edwards's biggest achievements was to sign an alliance with a Mongol Army that was also attacking Muslim forces.

A peace treaty was signed between the Christians and Muslims, then Edward returned to England after hearing the news that his father had died.

He was crowned King Edward in August 1274.

Crusades Trivia

The First Crusade was the most successful, and a big reason for this was that the Muslim world was disunited and suspicious of each other.

The battle cry of the Crusaders was 'Deus vult,' which means God wills it. The words come from the speech of the Pope gathering support for the First Crusade.

For Europeans, holding onto Jerusalem was more difficult than capturing it because Jerusalem was situated in the Middle East, which was some distance from Europe.

The word Crusade wasn't used until the 18th century to describe to Holy Wars. Crusade comes from the Latin word 'cruciata,' which means to mark with a cross.

At the time of the Crusades, the wars were referred to as 'peregrinatio,' or 'iter.' These words meant pilgrimage or journey.

The reason for the Crusades wasn't simply because of religion. The Crusades were often started for economic or political reasons.

The Catholic Church saw the Crusades as a means of extending the frontiers of its power. Kings and knights as a way of making money.

The Knights Templar was an order of military monks set up after the First Crusade to protect pilgrims to the Holy Land. Formed in poverty, the Knights Templar became famous for being skilled, well-trained fighters and very slick moneylenders and bankers. The order built a vast military and financial infrastructure that spanned Europe and the Middle East.

The Crusades caused a fusion between Christian and Islamic cultures leading to the end of the Dark Ages in Europe and the beginning of the Renaissance.

Although there were several unofficial Crusades, overall, there were nine major Crusades that attempted to capture Jerusalem. The Crusades took place over two hundred years and were the cause of millions of deaths.

One of the reasons why the Crusades stopped after two centuries was because Europe was going through a reformation, with religious groups turning their backs on the Pope and Catholicism. These

European Protestants, such as Martin Luther, had no time for the Crusades as they believed that they were not undertaken for religious reasons but as a power grab.

Crusades Quiz

1 Which city did the Seljuk Turks take control of in 1077?

2 What year was the first Crusade? Was it 1077, 1086, or 1096?

3 Which Crusade is also known as the Kings' Crusade?

4 What Christian city was attacked in the Fourth Crusade?

5 What Crusade was inspired by Stephen from Cloyes?

6 Who was the Sultan who agreed to a peace treaty with Richard the Lionheart?

7 Which French King died of dysentery near the city of Tunis?

8 Which future English King led the Ninth Crusade?

Thank you for Reading this Book

You can visit the English Reading Tree Page by clicking:

Visit Amazon's Keith Goodman Page (Mailing List)

Books in the English Reading Tree Series by Keith Goodman include:

The Titanic for Kids

Shark Facts for Kids

Solar System Facts for Kids

Dinosaur Facts for Kids

Save the Titanic for Kids

Discovering Ancient Egypt for Kids

Native American Culture for Kids

The American Civil War Explained for Kids

The American Revolution Explained for Kids

World War One in Brief for Kids

World War Two Explained for Kids

Middle Ages Facts and Trivia for kids

The Cold War Explained for Kids

The Great Depression and Stuff for Kids

Discovering Ancient Greece for Kids

The Vikings for Kids

The History of Ancient Weapons

Titanic Conspiracy Theories for Kids

The French Revolution Explained for Kids

The Bermuda Triangle Mystery for Kids

The Russian Revolution Explained for Kids

UFO Mysteries for Kids

Ancient Mesopotamia for Kids

Chinese Dynasties for Kids for Kids

Myths and Legends for Kids

The Loch Ness Monster for Kids

Ghost Stories for Kids

The Bigfoot Mystery for Kids

Unexplained Mysteries for Kids

The Vietnam War for Kids

The Knights Templar for Kids

The Crusades Explained for kids

Living History Series

1 Ancient Britain for Kids

2 Roman Britain for kids

3 Anglo-Saxon Britain for Kids

4 Viking Britain for Kids

5 Norman Britain for Kids

6 Plantagenet England for Kids

7 Tudor England for Kids

8 17th Century England for Kids

9 Georgian Britain for Kids

10 Victorian Britain for Kids

11 Britain at War for Kids

12 World War Two Britain for Kids

Crusades Quiz Answers

1 Jerusalem

2 1096

3 The Third Crusade

4 Constantinople

5 The Children's Crusade

6 Saladin

7 Louis IX of France

8 Lord Edward of England, who would later become King Edward I

Attributions

Getty, CC BY-SA 4.0 <https://creativecommons.org/licenses/by-sa/4.0>, via Wikimedia Commons

Crusade

Author and licence

https://commons.wikimedia.org/wiki/File:Crusade,_vers_1250.png

Printed in Great Britain
by Amazon